How Video Game Designers Use Math

By Jill Egan

Math Curriculum Consultant: Rhea A. Stewart, M.A.,
Specialist in Mathematics, Science,
and Technology Education

CHELSEA
CLUBHOUSE
An Imprint of Chelsea House Publishers

Math in the Real World: How Video Game Designers Use Math

Chelsea Clubhouse
An imprint of Chelsea House Publishers
132 West 31st Street
New York NY 10001

Library of Congress Cataloging-in-Publication Data
Egan, Jill.
        How video game designers use math / by Jill Egan; math curriculum consultant, Rhea A. Stewart.
            p. cm. — (Math in the real world)
        Includes index.
        ISBN 978-1-60413-603-6
        1. Computer games—Mathematics—Juvenile literature. 2. Computer animation—Mathematics—Juvenile literature. 3. Video games—Mathematics—Juvenile literature. 4. Computer games—Programming—Vocational guidance—Juvenile literature. 5. Video games—Design—Vocational guidance—Juvenile literature. I. Title.
        QA76.76.C672E33 2010
        794.801'51—dc22   2009024173

Chelsea Clubhouse books are available at special discounts when purchased in bulk quantities for businesses, associations, institutions, or sales promotions. Please call our Special Sales Department in New York at (212) 967-8800 or (800) 322-8755.

You can find Chelsea Clubhouse on the World Wide Web at http://www.chelseahouse.com

Developed for Chelsea House by RJF Publishing LLC (www.RJFpublishing.com)
Text and cover design by Tammy West/Westgraphix LLC
Illustrations by Spectrum Creative Inc.
Photo research by Edward A. Thomas
Index by Nila Glikin

Photo Credits: 4: © eStock Photo/Alamy; 6, 14: AP/Wide World Photos; 8, 12: iStockphoto; 16: Topic Photo Agency/age fotostock; 18: Godong/Photononstop/Photolibrary; 20: Corbis/Photolibrary; 22: © Gianni Muratore/Alamy; 24: AFP/Getty Images; 27: Jean Bernard/Tips Italia/Photolibrary.

Printed and bound in the United States of America

Bang RJF 10 9 8 7 6 5 4 3 2 1

This book is printed on acid-free paper.

All links and Web addresses were checked and verified to be correct at the time of publication. Because of the dynamic nature of the Web, some addresses and links may have changed since publication and may no longer be valid.

Table of Contents

Answers and helpful hints for the You Do the Math
activities are in the Answer Key.

Words that are defined in the Glossary are
in **bold** type the first time they appear in the text.

What Is Video Game Design?

Imagine spending your days getting paid to think about, create, and play video games. For video game designers, that's all in day's work!

There are many steps involved in creating a video game. It can take months, or even years, to create just one game.

Often, several designers will work together on developing a new game.

Designing the Game

First, video game designers have an idea for a game. They can get ideas from reading a favorite book, having fun outside, or playing other video games. Designers then might draw pictures to show their ideas. Or they might write about their ideas.

Next, they share their ideas with other video game designers. They talk about the different parts that make up a video game. They talk about **design**, **animation**, and sound effects. Now the designers are ready to create the game. They use computer software programs to build the game's graphics, characters, and sounds.

Math is one of the most important skills for a video game designer to have. For example, a designer might use **geometry** to draw a building.

A Video Game Designer's Schedule

The schedule below shows the number of days spent by one designer to develop a new game. Use the schedule to answer the questions.

A Designer's Schedule	
Task	**Days Spent on Task**
Coming up with the idea	June 1, 2
Meeting about the idea	June 3, 4, 5, 8, 9
Designing the characters	June 10, 11, 12, 15, 16, 17, 18, 19, 22, 23
Designing the scene	June 24, 25, 26, 29, 30, July 1, 2, 3
Designing the game's levels	July 6, 7, 8, 9, 10
Designing the sounds	July 13, 14, 15
Testing the game	July 16, 17, 20, 21

1. Which activity took the greatest number of days?

2. Which activity took the fewest number of days?

3. Which activity took more days: meeting about the idea or testing the game?

Designing for the Audience

Video game designers think about who plays the games they make. Players are called the audience. There are many features that make up a video game, including the characters, the type of game, and the speed of the game. Knowing what the audience likes can help designers plan the game.

What Does the Audience Want?

Designers look at different types of information to figure out what the audience likes. Designers look at **data** on charts, graphs, tables, and surveys. They use the data to learn about the people in the audience and their interests. Designers might look at a chart to find out if the audience would rather play sports games or fantasy games. Or they might read a survey to see if the audience would rather play a fast game or a slow one.

Video games with features the audience likes can be very successful. This shopper gets the last copy on a store's shelves of a popular game.

After video game designers know what the audience likes, they decide how to create the game to match the audience's interests.

Features People Liked Best

The bar graph shows the results when a video game company asked 100 people who had bought games before what features of video games they liked best. Use the graph to answer the questions.

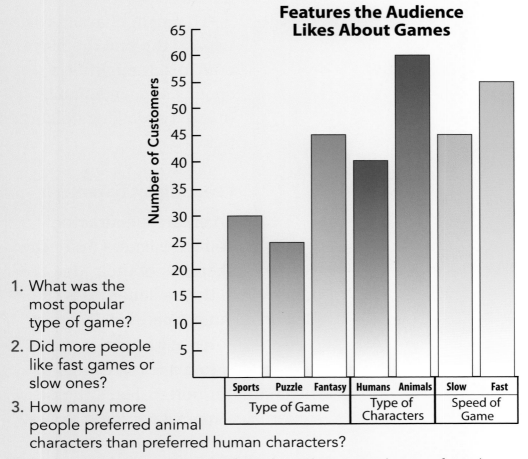

Features the Audience Likes About Games

1. What was the most popular type of game?

2. Did more people like fast games or slow ones?

3. How many more people preferred animal characters than preferred human characters?

4. How many fewer people preferred puzzle games than preferred fantasy games?

What a Character!

Think of some of the video games you have seen or played. What do you remember best about the games? There is a good chance it is the characters. Some video game characters are so popular that they appear in books, movies, and TV shows.

The main character is usually the one the player controls. It might be a space alien, an animal, or even a walking, talking pencil!

Using special software, designers can create detailed sketches of their characters on a computer screen.

Creating a Character

To create a character, some designers first draw sketches of their idea on paper. Next, the designer tests the idea on an audience. The designer uses the audience's comments and suggestions to make the design of the character better. Then, the designer uses special software to draw the character on a computer screen.

Some video game designers use geometry to help create characters.

They might want the character to look like a real person. They don't want the arms and legs to be too long or too short. Designers sometimes first draw a sketch of a body using shapes in geometry that are similar to parts of the body. For example, they might draw two long, narrow rectangles where the legs on a body go. The rectangles **represent** the legs.

Using shapes to represent body parts helps designers compare the sizes of objects to each other and keep the sizes in **proportion**. For example, a character's foot is going to be $\frac{1}{4}$ the length of the character's leg. If the designer's sketch uses a rectangle 4 inches long for the leg, then a rectangle 1 inch long for the foot will be in the correct proportion.

Knowing sizes in relation to each other helps designers later when it is time to draw the character moving or in different positions. They can go back to the rectangles to make sure the body's **dimensions**, or measurements, are still accurate.

You Do the Math

Arms and Legs

A designer is sketching a character. The length of the character's arms will be $\frac{3}{4}$ the length of the legs. If the designer's sketch uses a 4-inch-long rectangle for each leg, how long should the rectangle be that the designer uses for each arm?

Creating a Scene

Characters don't just run around a blank screen. They move through a background, or scene, that is designed to show the setting the character is in. The scene helps create the feeling, or **mood**, of the game.

If the scene is in a happy, upbeat game, the designers probably won't choose to create a dark, nighttime scene with fog rolling through. That wouldn't match the mood of the game. A scene that is bright and sunny would match the mood of the game better.

Designing the Action

After the designers know what kind of scene they want to create, they draw a map of the scene. This helps designers see how the game will be played. They can see how a character will move through the game. Just as someone might follow a map to get from one part of town to another, designers want to have a map so that they know how the character is going to get from one part of the game to another.

Getting From Here to There

The map below, called a grid map, is like the kind of map a video game designer might make. Each column is named by a letter. Each row is named by a number. Each box is named by the letter and number for its column and row. For example, the box where Spring Lake is located is in column C and row 1. Spring Lake is in box (C, 1). The letter and number (C, 1) are called the coordinates of the box. The map also has a compass rose that shows which way is north, south, east, and west. Use the map and the compass rose to answer the questions.

1. What are the coordinates for the box where the supermarket is located?

2. What building is located in the box with coordinates (C, 3)?

3. In which direction would you travel to get from the bank to the supermarket?

4. What building is located in the box with coordinates (G, 2)?

5. To get from the school to the park, in which direction would you travel?

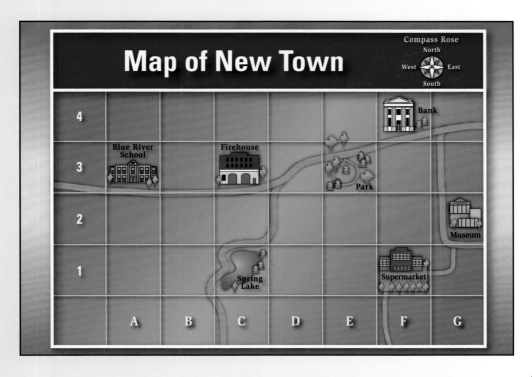

All About Animation

Close your eyes and move your arm in a circle. What did you notice? Did your arm stay straight or did your elbow bend? Video game designers pay close attention to the exact movements of people, animals, and objects to help them create a game's animation—the movement of characters and objects on the screen. A person who creates animation is called an animator.

Keeping It Real

Animators watch how our legs move when we run or how a ball bounces across a room. When they design games, they use their observations to help them make movements look **realistic**. They try to imitate real-life

Video game designers watch how people move when they are active. This helps the designers make the movements of their game characters realistic.

movement on the video screen. Animators can spend days working to get the movement of something just right.

Create a Flip Book

You can make your own animation with a flip book. You will need 6 sheets of paper of the same size and a clip to hold the left edges together like a book.

Here's how to make your flip book.

1. Number each page in the upper right corner, from 1 to 6.

2. On each sheet of paper, copy the grid shown here.

4						
3						
2						
1						
	A	B	C	D	E	F

3. Start with a simple object: a bouncing ball. Draw it with a pencil first. You can color the pictures in later. Keep the ball the same size in each picture.

4. On the page numbered 1, draw the ball in the box with coordinates (A, 1).

5. On page 2, draw the ball in (B,2).

6. On each following page, draw the ball in (C, 3), (D, 2), (E, 1), and (F, 2).

7. When you are finished drawing, clip the pages together on the left side. Make sure the pages are in order from 1 to 6.

8. Holding your book on the left side, use the thumb of your right hand to flip through the pages quickly to see the ball bouncing across the pages.

After you've mastered this flip book, you can try making one that is more difficult by adding a background scene, creating a moving character, or adding more pages.

Thinking About Speed

Imagine a horse walking across a meadow. Now, picture it running from a fire-breathing dragon. The horse in your imagination probably moved faster when it was being chased by the dragon. Designers think about speed when they create video games. Speed is how fast or slow an object moves. When characters or objects move across the screen, designers try to make the speed seem realistic. They also try to make the speed fit the type of game. In a basketball game, they make the players move up and down the court quickly. In a puzzle game, the speed might be slower.

Basketball players run down the court quickly. In a basketball video game, the designers will make the characters move quickly so the game will be realistic.

Getting Up to Speed

To help them know what speed to use, designers **observe** the speed of things around them. If they are designing a game about a bird, they want to know how fast or slow birds move at different times. Designers might watch a bird slowly flying in circles above a lake. Then, they might observe how the bird speeds up and dives down toward the water to catch a fish. The speed of a person, animal, or thing in real life and speed on a computer screen are a bit different. Designers must **estimate** to help them figure out how fast or slow something should move on the screen to look realistic.

You Do the Math

How Well Can You Estimate?

How well can you estimate time? Here are three activities:

1. Bounce a ball 10 times
2. Write your first name 10 times
3. Sit down and stand up 8 times

On a sheet of paper, make three columns. At the top of the left column, write Activity. At the top of the center column, write Estimated Time. At the top of the right column, write Actual Time. List the three activities in the left column. Then, in the center column, write down how many seconds you think each activity should take you to complete. These are your estimated times. Next, do each activity, and time yourself or have someone time you with a watch, clock, or stopwatch. Write down in the Actual Time column how long each activity took. Now compare your estimated and actual times. How close was each estimate to the actual time?

Creating Color

The first home video games were introduced more than 30 years ago. These games were in black and white. The first color video games were sold with a colored plastic sheet that players taped to their TV screen to add color to the game. Today's games are much different. Color is an important part of video game design.

Color is a way designers create excitement or mystery. Designers might choose the color red to show that something is hot. Or they might choose blue to show that something is cold.

Designers use computer software to create colors and many other aspects of video games.

Making the Color

Designers mix different amounts of just a few colors to create all the colors they need. Red, yellow, and blue are called primary colors. Mixing different amounts of two or all three of the primary colors creates the colors you see on the screen. Adding black makes a color darker, and adding white makes a color lighter.

Designers give each of the basic colors they work with a certain **code** that represents the color. Next they put those codes into computer software. Then, they mix the color codes using the software to create new colors. They work hard to get colors exactly the way they want them.

Putting It Together

In this diagram, R, Y, and B are the codes for the primary colors red, yellow, and blue. Mixing two primary colors together makes a secondary color. Orange, violet, and green are the secondary colors. Red mixed with yellow makes orange. Red mixed with blue makes violet. Yellow mixed with blue makes green. In the diagram the codes for the secondary colors are O, V, and G. Use the diagram and the codes to fill in the missing letter in each of these **equations**.

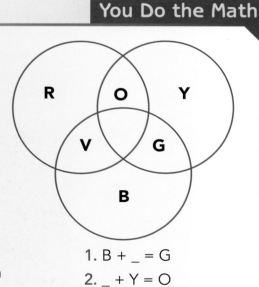

1. B + _ = G
2. _ + Y = O
3. R + B = _

What's That Sound?

Have you ever watched a TV program with the sound turned off? Probably not. Without sound and music, a TV program, movie, or video game isn't as exciting.

A person who creates the sound and music for a video game is called a sound designer. Sound designers use music and sound effects to create excitement and mood.

Types of Sounds

Music is the tune that plays in the background during a game. Sounds are heard at certain times in a game. You might hear the sound of a crowd

Earphones help the girl playing this game enjoy the music and sound effects without disturbing others.

cheering. Or you might hear the sound of a bell ringing when a player gets a reward.

Sound designers decide how the music or sounds will change to fit different events in a game. At the beginning of a game, the music might be quiet. As a player gets closer to reaching a goal, the music might get louder. Designers can use graphing to match the sounds and music to what is happening in a game. The graphs help them see the points during a game at which different sounds and music are needed.

Graphing Sound

A sound designer created this line graph to show three points in a game when the character reaches a goal and the music should get much louder. Each point on the graph is named by the letter of the vertical line and the number of the horizontal line that cross at that point. The first point is where lines A and 1 cross. The coordinates for this point are (A, 1). What are the coordinates for the 3 points where the music gets much louder than at other times?

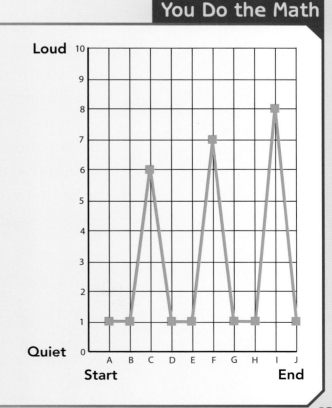

On the Level

Most video games have different sections, which are called levels. Like the chapters of a book, the different levels together make a whole game. The person who creates the levels is called the level designer. Level designers think of each level as a small game within a whole game.

Planning the Levels

Levels are one of the ways games keep players interested. Level designers try to make each level challenging and fun. If a level is too easy or too hard, players might not be interested in continuing the game.

Players must complete certain **tasks** at each level before they can move on to the next one. To complete the tasks, players have to make choices. If players make the best choices, they will get to the next level faster or more easily. Usually, each level is harder than the one before it.

The challenge of moving from one level to the next adds to the excitement of many video games.

Moving Up in the Game

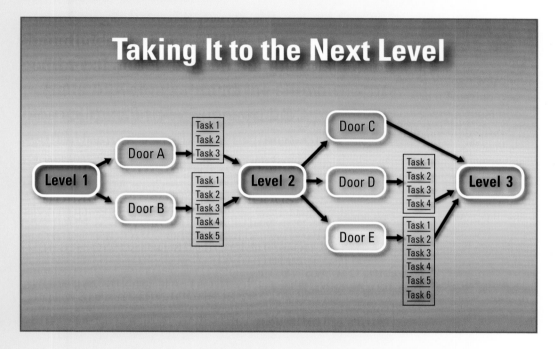

Taking It to the Next Level

The diagram shows the different levels of a game. At each level the player has to choose which door to go through. Each door leads to a different number of tasks that the player must complete before getting to the next level. Use the diagram to answer the questions.

1. Which door has the fewest number of tasks to get from Level 1 to Level 2?

2. Which combination of doors gives the fewest tasks to get from Level 1 to Level 3?

3. How many tasks in all do you have to complete if you choose doors A and E?

4. Which is the only door that gets a player to the next level without having to complete any tasks?

3-D Design

When people look at something, their eyes are able to see three different dimensions of an object: its length, its width, and its height or depth. Something that has three dimensions is often called 3-D for short.

If we see a picture of a penny next to a real penny, we can tell which object is the real penny just by looking. Our eyes see the height of the penny's edge. We see how light hits the raised parts of Abraham Lincoln's face differently from the way it hits the flat picture of the penny. Flat images that have only length and width are called 2-dimensional, or 2-D, images.

Video game designers work hard to make objects in a game look 3-D.

Using 3-D in Video Games

Video games are played on a flat screen, but designers make things in the games look 3-D. Designers use 3-D design to make the game more realistic to the players. They use geometry to create shapes that look as if they have three dimensions. To the players, it looks as if they could, for example, catch a 3-D toad hopping across the screen. The designers also use shading to create the look of shadows and light. This makes an object seem even more realistic.

Creating Depth

The shape on the left is a rectangle. It has two dimensions, length and width. The object on the right is called a rectangular prism. It has three dimensions, length, width, and height. The rectangular prism has six different faces. The drawing shows three of those faces. One looks like the front of the box. One looks like a side of the box, and one looks like the top. On a piece of paper, draw each of the three faces you see on the rectangular prism.

Capturing Motion

Sometimes the smile or the wink of a character in a game is so realistic, it's hard to tell that you're looking at an animated figure. One way designers create realistic characters is by using something called motion capture. It helps them create lifelike movements based on a real person's movements.

Using Motion Capture in Video Games

In motion capture, a person wears a suit with devices on it called **electronic markers**. As the person moves, the markers **track** the person's movements and send information to a computer. The movements are recorded using computer software. The software then creates a digital image of the body's movements that can be used in creating animation.

Even though a computer records the body's movements, the designer must make the software work. The designer creates equations that will give the computer directions to chart

The movements of this model wearing electronic markers are captured on a computer screen.

the body's movements and to store the information in a digital format. The designer then uses this information to help make an animated figure move in realistic ways.

Charting Movement

In the illustrations below, the green dots show places where a person would have electronic markers in a motion-capture suit. Look at how the markers on the right ankle and knee change position from the left picture, showing a person standing still, to the right picture, showing a person climbing a step. Capturing that motion in computer software helps a designer make an animated character look realistic climbing stairs.

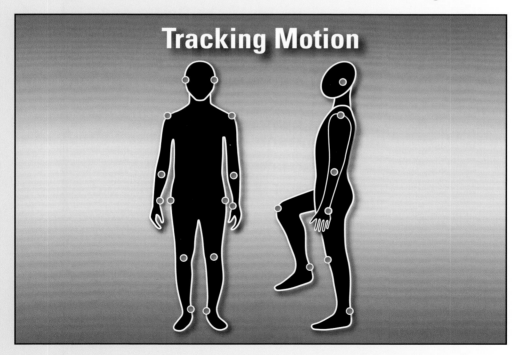

Tracking Motion

Draw your own stick figures with electronic markers. Describe how the markers on the right wrist and elbow change position as your "person" raises his or her right arm to throw a ball.

25

Meet Satoshi Tajiri

Video game designer Satoshi Tajiri grew up near Tokyo, the capital city of the country of Japan. As a boy, he had a hobby that later inspired him to create a video game that became famous. Tajiri collected bugs. He collected as many different kinds of bugs as he could find. He traded the bugs with his friends. He also enjoyed playing video games.

From Player to Designer

When he was older, Tajiri became frustrated when he couldn't find games he wanted to play. He decided to make his own. In 1990, he came up with the idea of Pokémon. Pokémon, also known as Pocket Monsters, is one of the most popular video games of all time. The theme, "Gotta Catch 'Em All," goes back to when Tajiri was a boy and tried to catch all the bugs he could. Tajiri says that all of the things he did as a child helped him create Pokémon.

Today, Tajiri continues to create new versions of the game. He spends different parts of his day working on his ideas in different ways. His hard work has made Pokémon one of the most well-known video games in the world.

Video game designers often put in many hours a day at their computers.

You Do the Math

A Day in the Life of a Video Game Designer

Video game designers have busy days. The schedule below shows how one designer spent an 8-hour workday. Use the schedule to figure out what fraction of the time the designer spent on different tasks in the 8-hour day. Example: What fraction of the designer's day was spent brainstorming? The answer is $\frac{1}{8}$, because the designer spent one hour (1:30 P.M. to 2:30 P.M.) out of an 8-hour day brainstorming.

A Video Game Designer's Day	
Time	**Activity**
9:00 A.M. – 10:30 A.M.	Meeting about future games
10:30 A.M. – 1:00 P.M.	Working on game design
1:00 P.M. – 1:30 P.M.	Lunch
1:30 P.M. – 2:30 P.M.	Brainstorming new game ideas with other designers
2:30 P.M. – 4:30 P.M.	Meeting with testers
4:30 P.M. – 5:00 P.M.	Working on game design

1. What fraction of the day was spent working on game design?

2. What fraction of the day was spent meeting with testers?

If You Want to Be a Video Game Designer

Do video games interest you? Maybe a career in video game design is right for you.

If you're interested in video game design as a career, there are summer camps and after-school programs that train young designers. When it's time to go to college, there are many schools that offer courses in video game design or animation. Many designers choose to study digital art or computer technology. They may have careers as animators, level designers, or sound designers, or they may work in other aspects of game design.

If you are the type of person who likes to solve problems, works well as a part of a team, and likes to think creatively, then you might be the type of person who makes a good video game designer. Designers need skills in math and computer technology, and it's never too early to start learning as much about these areas as possible. Of course, an important part of being a video game designer is to love to play video games!

Answer Key

Pages 4–5: What Is Video Game Design?:

1. Designing the characters (10 days). **2.** Coming up with the idea (2 days). **3.** Meeting about the idea. This activity took 5 days (June 3, 4, 5, 8, 9). Testing the game took 4 days (July 16, 17, 20, 21).

Pages 6–7: Designing for the Audience:

1. Fantasy games. **2.** Fast games. **3.** 20 (60 people preferred animal characters; 40 people preferred human characters; $60 - 40 = 20$). **4.** 20 (25 people preferred puzzle games; 45 people preferred fantasy games; $45 - 25 = 20$).

Pages 8–9: What a Character!:

3 inches ($\frac{3}{4} \times 4 = \frac{12}{4}$; $\frac{12}{4} = 3$).

Pages 10–11: Creating a Scene:

1. (F, 1). **2.** The firehouse. **3.** South. **4.** The museum. **5.** East.

Pages 12–13: All About Animation:

The 6 pages of your flip book should look like this:

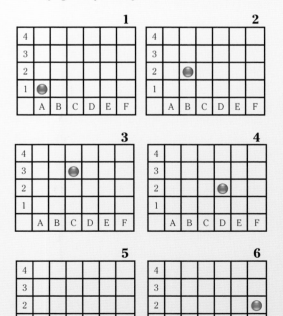

Pages 14–15: Thinking About Speed:

Sample answer: your table might look like this:

How Much Time Activities Take		
Activity	**Estimated Time**	**Actual Time**
Bounce a ball 10 times	20 seconds	16 seconds
Write your first name 10 times	15 seconds	20 seconds
Sit down and stand up 8 times	10 seconds	11 seconds

Pages 16–17: Creating Color:

1. Y. **2.** R. **3.** V.

Pages 18–19: What's That Sound?:

The coordinates are (C, 6), (F, 7), and (I, 8).

Pages 20–21: On the Level:

1. Door A. **2.** Doors A and C. **3.** 9 tasks (3 tasks for Door A + 6 tasks for Door E = 9 tasks). **4.** Door C.

Pages 22–23: 3-D Design:

Pages 24–25: Capturing Motion:

The markers on the right wrist and elbow, which would be almost straight down from the right shoulder marker when the person is standing still, move up to be at about the same level as the right shoulder marker when the person is throwing a ball.

Page 26–27: Meet Satoshi Tajiri:

1. The designer spent $\frac{3}{8}$ of the day working on game design (3 hours out of an 8-hour day); 10:30 A.M. to 1:00 P.M. is $2\frac{1}{2}$ hours, and 4:30 P.M. to 5:00 P.M. is $\frac{1}{2}$ hour; $2\frac{1}{2} + \frac{1}{2} = 3$. **2.** The designer spent $\frac{2}{8}$ of the day meeting with testers (2:30 P.M. to 4:30 P.M. is 2 hours); $\frac{2}{8}$ can also be written $\frac{1}{4}$.

Glossary

animation—Using drawings to give life, motion, or activity to characters on a screen.

code—A system of symbols, letters, or numbers used to represent information.

data—Information that is collected about a topic.

design—A plan for how something will be made.

dimension—A measurement of something in one direction, such as length, width, or height.

electronic markers—Sensors that track a body's movement and send signals to a computer.

equation—A mathematical statement showing that two things are equal.

estimate—To figure out about how many or how much.

geometry—The part of math that is about lines, angles, shapes, and solid figures.

mood—The feeling created by a story's setting.

observe—To see or notice something while watching carefully.

proportion—The size or extent of something in relation to something else.

realistic—Seeming to be real.

represent—To stand for something else.

task—A job or mission.

track—To watch or to record the progress or movement of something.

To Learn More

Read these books:

Cunningham, Kevin. *Cool Careers: Video Game Designer*. Ann Arbor, Mich.: Cherry Lake Publishing, 2009.

Duffield, Katy. *Ken Kutaragi: PlayStation Developer*. San Diego, Calif.: KidHaven Press, 2007.

Ferguson's Careers in Focus: Computer and Video Game Design. New York: Facts On File, 2005.

Mortensen, Lori. *Satoshi Tajiri: Pokémon Creator*. San Diego, Calif.: KidHaven Press, 2009.

Look up these Web sites:

Aniboom—Create Your Own Animation
http://www.aniboom.com/Animachines

DragonflyTV: Real Scientists: David Ortiz
http://www.pbskids.org/dragonflytv/scientists/scientist15.html

The Video Game Revolution: History
http://www.pbs.org/kcts/videogamerevolution/history

Key Internet search terms:

animation, computer-assisted design, video game design

Index

About the Author

Jill Egan is a freelance writer who has written numerous stories about the events and people who shape our world. A native of Juneau, Alaska, she currently lives with her husband in San Francisco, California.